Cambridge Discover

Level 3

Series editor: Nicholas Tims

Scotland

Richard MacAndrew

CAMBRIDGE
UNIVERSITY PRESS

CAMBRIDGE UNIVERSITY PRESS
Cambridge, New York, Melbourne, Madrid, Cape Town,
Singapore, São Paulo, Delhi, Tokyo, Mexico City

Cambridge University Press
c/Orense, 4 – 13°, 28020 Madrid, Spain

www.cambridge.org
Information on this title: www.cambridge.org/9788483235799

First published 2009
Third reprint 2011

Richard MacAndrew has asserted his right to be identified as the Author of the Work
in accordance with the Copyright, Design and Patents Act 1988.

Printed in Spain by Gráficas Varona, S.A.

ISBN 978-84-832-3579-9 Paperback; legal deposit: S.934-2009
ISBN 978-84-832-3576-8 Paperback with audio CD/CD-ROM pack for Windows, Mac
and Linux; legal deposit: S.225-2009

No character in this work is based on any person living or dead.
Any resemblance to an actual person or situation is purely accidental.

*To the memory of William McAndrew of Elgin (1752–1819), who left home at the age
of eighteen to seek his fortune.*

Illustrations by Sebastijan Camagajevac (Beehive Illustration) and El Ojo del Huracán

Audio recording by BraveArts, S.L.

The publishers are grateful to the following for permission to reproduce photographic
material on the cover: istockphoto.com/©Theo Fitzhugh; istockphoto.com/©nojustice;
©Orion9nl/Dreamstime.com; istockphoto.com/©generacionx; istockphoto.com/
©sumnersgraphicsinc; istockphoto.com/©myrrha; shutterstock/©Monkey Business Images

The paper that this book has been printed on is produced using an elemental
chlorine-free (ECF) process at mills registered to ISO14001 (2004), the environmental
management standard. The mills source their wood fibre from sustainably-managed
forests. No hardwood pulp is used in the production of this paper.

Contents

Introduction

Scotland has many different faces. It has busy cities, quiet islands, mountains, lochs (the Scottish word for 'lake') and large areas of beautiful and empty countryside. It has Highland Games, Highland dancing, bagpipes and traditional[1] music. It has strange and dark stories from history and beyond. And there is present-day Scotland, a small but dynamic country, with its own special character and identity. Traditions and history come together with new ideas from the young Scots of today to make Scotland an exciting and modern country.

Facts about Scotland ───────────────

- The population of Scotland is just over five million.
- The capital city is Edinburgh with a population of over 450,000.
- The largest city is Glasgow with a population of about 600,000.
- The other main towns include Aberdeen, Dundee, Inverness and Stirling.
- Scotland has an area of 78,772 square kilometres.
- There are just under eight hundred islands in Scotland. People live on about ninety-five of these islands.
- Three languages are spoken in Scotland: English, Scots and Gaelic. Everyone speaks English. However, about 30% of the population also speak Scots; and about 1.5% speak Gaelic – that is just under sixty thousand people.
- The word 'Gaelic' refers only to the language, not to the people.
- The highest mountain in Scotland is Ben Nevis.

A language note

The country is Scotland. The people are 'Scots', or 'Scotsmen' and 'Scotswomen', or 'Scottish men' and 'Scottish women'. The adjective is 'Scottish'. There is an adjective 'Scotch', but it is only used for whisky, pancakes and a few other dishes!

Chapter 1

Wild Scotland

There are mountains in the north of Scotland and on the islands off the west coast. This area, almost two-thirds of the country, is often called 'the Highlands and Islands'. It is one of the loneliest places in Europe: fewer people live here per square kilometre than almost anywhere else in Europe. Yet it is from this area that much of 'traditional' Scotland comes: traditional music and dance, the Highland Games, clans and tartans, and the Gaelic language.

The Highlands

Scotland has mountains. They are not mountains like the Himalayas – or even the Alps. But they are mountains – and the ten highest mountains in Scotland are also the ten highest mountains in Great Britain. Some of them are rocky; some are green. You can walk and climb in the summer; you can ski in the winter. They can look beautiful and inviting, but in bad weather they can be dangerous places.

Ben Nevis is Scotland's highest mountain at 1,344 metres. Although there is a path all the way to the top, it is not always an easy climb. For most of the year the wind at the top is very strong; there is cloud at the top six days out of seven; and even in the middle of summer there can be snow. Sixty to seventy times a year the mountain rescue team is called out to help walkers and climbers who have got into difficulty. Over the last ten years, twenty-two people have died on the mountain.

Munros

At the end of the 19th century Sir Hugh Munro, who belonged to the Scottish Mountaineering Club, made a list of all the Scottish mountains over 3,000 feet (914 metres) in height. There are 284 of them. These mountains became known as the 'Munros' and very quickly it became a hobby to climb them all. Over four thousand people, both young and old, have climbed them all and the number rises every year.

Four-year-old wants to be top

Four-year-old Darwin Bradley from Guisborough in the north of England wants to become the youngest person to climb all Scotland's 284 Munros. He climbed his first at the age of twenty-two months and has so far completed fifteen.

Sarah Bradley, aged thirty-two and Darwin's mum, said, 'He absolutely loves it. We've always been interested in walking.

When he was twenty-two months old we were on holiday and we just thought we'd see if he could make it up a mountain. We did the walk in eight hours and Darwin had a sleep at the top.'

Darwin already has plans for when he has completed all the Munros.

'I want to throw snowballs from Mount Everest,' he says.

Walks in the mountains

There are a number of long walks through the mountains in Scotland. Possibly the most famous of these is the West Highland Way. It is 152 kilometres long and goes from Milngavie (near Glasgow) to Fort William in the Highlands. About fifty thousand people do this walk every year. It takes about six or seven days.

If you're still feeling strong, you can continue from Fort William, along the side of Loch Ness, to Inverness. This walk is called the Great Glen Way. It is a further 117 kilometres and will take another five or six days.

The islands

There are over 750 islands off the coast of Scotland, but people live on only about 95 of them. Lewis and Harris is the largest island. The north part of the island is called Lewis and the south part Harris. Often people talk as if they are two islands, but they are not. Lewis and Harris has a population of almost twenty thousand, but there are around twenty-five islands where ten or even fewer people live.

Life can be difficult in the Highlands and islands: villages are small and far apart and the winters can be hard and very cold. Because of this, the people who live there are generally friendly, welcoming and caring. In the villages it will be the tourists, not the locals, who lock their cars when they leave them.

Lonely schoolgirl wants classmates

Caroline Mackinnon, the loneliest schoolgirl in Britain, is hoping that she will soon have some classmates. Caroline is one of the fifteen people who live on the island of Canna off the west coast of Scotland, and she is the only student in the island's school.

'There are people to play with when I'm on holiday,' says Caroline, 'but at school there are no people to play with. It would be good if there were kids here.'

Canna is seven kilometres long by 1.5 kilometres wide. The nearest shop is four hours away by boat; the nearest doctor is a little closer on the island of Eigg.

There are two empty houses on the island and islanders are hoping that new families will come to live there. There has been interest from all around the world including Dubai, Japan and Australia.

However, Caroline's aunt, Winnie Mackinnon, warns that life is not easy on Canna. 'Winters are long, dark and can be hard for those not used to it,' she says.

Obviously not all schools are as small as Caroline Mackinnon's. In Scotland the average size of a secondary school is just over eight hundred students. Schools in the Highlands, though, are often smaller because there are fewer people in the area. Gairloch High School on the west coast has about two hundred pupils. And some students have to travel as far as sixty kilometres to get there. The school has four coaches and three minibuses to bring them to school in the morning and to take them home in the evening.

Most jobs for teens in the Highlands and on the islands are in tourism – in hotels and restaurants, for example. Towns and villages are very quiet during the winter months, but busier during the summer when visitors come to experience the wild countryside and the beautiful coast.

Crofting

A croft is a kind of small farm found only in the Highlands and islands of Scotland. There are about eighteen thousand crofts in the area. A crofter – the person who farms on the croft – keeps a few cows and sheep, and grows some vegetables. However, because the land is so poor, crofters cannot always make enough money from farming. They often have to do other work as well as looking after their croft.

The Standing Stones of Calanais _____

England has Stonehenge, France has Carnac. Scotland has Calanais – stones that you will never forget. These stones are called 'standing stones' and they were put in place a long time before history began.

The village of Calanais is on wild and faraway Lewis. There are three main groups of stones in and near the village. The largest and most famous is a group of fifty stones, thirteen of them in a circle, with the others in rows going north, south, east and west.

The stones are between three and five thousand years old and they seem to point in some way to the sun and the stars. Some people think that they were an early way for farmers to work out the right time for the different jobs they had to do.

Because the island is so far away, there are few visitors to Calanais. But if you make the journey, you will be happy you did. You can stand among the stones, look out over the sea and the hills and hear nothing but the wind. If you are there at sunrise or sunset, it will be an experience you will remember all your life.

The 'airport' at Barra

Barra is one of the many islands off the west coast of Scotland. It is 6.5 kilometres wide, and 13 kilometres long and just over a thousand people live there. Barra has one of only two beach airports in the world. The other one is in Australia. Planes land and take off on a sandy beach on the north of the island. The flight times are always changing because of the sea. When the sea comes in and covers the beach, no planes can land.

Scottish wildlife

red deer

otter

red squirrel

puffin

golden eagle

The Scottish mountains and islands are home to some wonderful wildlife including deer, otters and squirrels. The red deer is the largest of these. It can stand 1.3 metres high and weigh 126 kilos. Otters live on land and sea. They can live in both fresh water and sea water. They generally eat fish; but they also look for food on land, eating mice and even rabbits. Squirrels live in the forests and Scotland is one of the few places in Britain where you can still find red squirrels.

There are also some interesting birds. The puffin is the most unusual-looking bird in Scotland. It looks a bit like a small penguin, but it flies well. The largest bird in Scotland is the golden eagle. It can be one metre tall and has very wide wings. For a time there were almost no golden eagles left in Scotland, but their numbers are growing and people are not allowed to shoot them any more.

Eilidh MacFadyen's story ─────────

Eilidh MacFadyen comes from the island of Tiree. Her first language is Gaelic and she learnt English at school. Read what she has to say about growing up in the Highlands and islands.

Growing up on Tiree

Tiree is a great place to grow up. It's safe, quiet and beautiful. It might not have things that the big towns and cities have, but it has the countryside instead. Tiree hasn't got a swimming pool or a shopping centre – but you can swim in the sea and you enjoy shopping centres more when you leave the island.

Tiree has got a lot of crofts. One of my favourite times of year is spring because there are lots of lambs[2] around. I like going out and helping my dad during lambing time, and enjoy giving food to the lambs.

On Tiree we go to school when we are three years old. That's when I started at the Gaelic

16

playgroup. It was really fun, and I met the kids I later went to school with. The following year I went to primary school. There were two groups in the primary school: Gaelic and English. I was the youngest in the school when I started. There were only five people in my Gaelic group, and I was the only girl. The English and the Gaelic groups did music, PE and art together – just seven of us in the class. Then, in the third year, I started to learn English.

Moving to secondary school was really easy, because the primary and secondary schools share the same building. Tiree is such a small island that we knew many of the teachers before going to secondary school.

Living on an island means we go on quite a lot of school trips. One of my favourite trips was the Youth Games trip. This was a sporting trip. There were lots of different competitions, and Tiree was in the hockey and football competitions.

I was in the hockey team. We came second out of seven teams. Because I was in a class with four boys during primary school, I played a lot of sport – and I love it.

Tiree is a very musical island. And we're lucky because we have some really good teachers. I started playing the accordion when I was ten. You can also learn the piano, the violin, the flute, the pipes, the drums and other instruments. I love going to school on Tiree because everyone knows each other and we are all friends.

ACTIVITIES

1 Complete the sentences with information from Chapter 1.

1 One of the least populated areas of Europe is *the Highlands and Islands* .

2 The highest mountain in Scotland is ....

3 All the mountains in Scotland more than 914 metres high are called the ....

4 The biggest Scottish island is ....

5 There are some very old stones, which were possibly used to tell the time, in ....

6 There is an unusual airport at ....

2 Complete the sentences with the names in the box.

> Darwin Bradley   Eilidh MacFadyen
> Caroline Mackinnon   ~~Sir Hugh Munro~~

1 *Sir Hugh Munro* has a group of mountains named after him.

2 .... slept at the top of a mountain.

3 .... doesn't have any classmates.

4 .... likes her school and where she lives.

3 Answer the questions.

1 What can make life difficult in the Highlands and Islands?

   Villages are far apart and winters can be hard and cold.

2 What jobs do most teens in the Highlands and Islands do?

   ....

3 Where do otters live?

   ....

Chapter 2

Traditional Scotland

When people think of Scotland, they think of many things, for example, tartan, bagpipes, kilts, and people speaking English with a different accent. Here we look at some of the traditional ideas about Scotland, and try to find out what is fact and what is not.

What is a clan?

'Clan' is a Gaelic word meaning 'children' or 'family'. A clan in Scotland is a large family or group of families. There is a clan leader called a 'chief', and traditionally the people in the clan did what the chief told them. Clans were more important in the Highlands than other parts of Scotland. There was often fighting between different clans. They fought over land or the animals they used to farm. Sometimes the fighting continued for many years. During the 17th and 18th centuries a lot of people moved away from the Highlands. As a result, the clans became less important. Today there are still clans and clan chiefs in Scotland, but not in the traditional way.

What is Gaelic?

Scottish Gaelic /ˈgælɪk/ is the oldest language used in Scotland, but today it is spoken by just under sixty thousand people. As a language, it is very similar to Irish Gaelic /ˈgeɪlɪk/. Most Gaelic speakers in Scotland live in the Highlands or the Western Isles. In recent years the number of Gaelic speakers has grown. These days Gaelic is taught in schools and there are Gaelic TV programmes and Gaelic pop bands.

Here are some Gaelic words:

Alba /ˈæləpæ/ — Scotland
ceilidh /ˈkeɪli/ — an evening of singing and dancing
compuitear /komˈpjuːtə/ — computer
fòn-laimh /fəʊnˈlaɪv/ — mobile phone

What is a kilt?

The kilt is generally thought of as traditional Scottish clothing. In fact, it used to be traditional only in the Highlands. Now it is worn all over Scotland. People wear them like a skirt. And men and boys wear them too!

Do Scots wear kilts every day? Generally speaking, no. People wear kilts when they want to look good – for example at parties and for weddings. And people sometimes wear kilts when they want other people to know they are Scottish – for example, when they go to international football or rugby matches.

What is tartan?

Tartan is the name given to the pattern[3] that you usually find on kilts. Tartan is also used for all sorts of other things: skirts, trousers, scarves and so on. In early times people wore any kind of tartan they liked. However, from the 19th century, different clans decided to have their own tartans – so if your name was MacGregor, you wore the MacGregor tartan.

What are bagpipes?

No one knows how or when the bagpipes first came to Scotland, but they quickly became the traditional form of Scottish music. There are many different kinds of pipes both in Scotland and in other countries. In Scotland the most popular kind is the Highland bagpipe or 'the Great Pipe'. They can be played in a band of pipes and drums, and people also play them on their own. You will often see a piper on a city street playing so that people give money.

Bodega – new Scottish music rocks US festival

The young band that came on next certainly got the place rocking. Bodega are a five-piece band who come from different parts of the Highlands and islands of Scotland. They only got together in their late teens and have not been playing as a band that long. But as soon as they hit the first notes, I knew we were in for a great time. Bodega mix traditional Gaelic music with American folk songs and some of their own songs. They play the guitar, violin, bagpipes and many other strange and interesting instruments. They sing in Gaelic and in English. It is traditional music – but traditional music with a difference. They could, and should, be the next big thing. They have already played in France, Italy, Norway and the US, as well as the UK. Catch them if you can!

What is a ceilidh?

Ceilidh is a Gaelic word that means 'visit'. In the past people would get together in someone's house and tell stories and poems. Today the word usually means an evening of singing and dancing.

What is a Burns supper?

Robert Burns was a famous Scottish poet. He wrote poems and songs in both Scots and English. On 25 January, all over the world, Scots people have a traditional Burns supper to remember Robert Burns. At a Burns supper, there is usually a piper who plays. The guests eat a type of food called haggis and drink whisky. And some of Burns' poems are read and sung.

What is Hogmanay?

One thing the Scots do well is have a party. And the biggest and best Scottish parties are at Hogmanay. 'Hogmanay' is the word the Scots use for New Year's Eve or 31 December. Parties for young and old will start early in the evening. Then at midnight, everyone sings *Auld Lang Syne*, a Robert Burns song. Scots often then go and visit their friends and neighbours to wish them a Happy New Year. This is called 'first-footing' – because you are often the first person to set foot inside the house of the friend or neighbour in the New Year. Traditionally your first visitor of the New Year should bring presents of coal[4] (to give heat), something to eat (traditionally shortbread, a type of biscuit) and something to drink (traditionally whisky).

What is whisky?

Whisky is the Scottish national drink and has been made in Scotland for longer than anyone can remember. Whisky is made in many other countries too – for example in Ireland, America, India and Japan. But any Scot will tell you that Scotch whisky is the best. In 2006 an eighty-year-old bottle of Scotch whisky was sold in New York for $20,000 – but it is not usually as expensive as that!

What is Haggis?

Haggis is probably the most famous Scottish food. There are many different recipes for haggis – today you can even get a vegetarian haggis. However, a traditional haggis will include the heart, liver and lungs of a sheep, onion, oats, and spices.

The ingredients are cut into very small pieces and mixed together. Traditionally they were cooked in a sheep's stomach. At one time, because it was made from very cheap meat, haggis was eaten by the poor. Today you can find it everywhere, even in the best restaurants.

Fast food

Although there is some excellent food in Scotland, you can also find a large number of different fast foods. Fish and chips, called a 'fish supper' in Scotland, is popular. So too are baked potatoes. But there are also some strange fast foods. Most of them are deep fried in oil. How about deep-fried pizza? Or deep-fried banana? You can also find deep-fried pieces of pineapple, even deep-fried ice cream. But the most famous of

these unusual fast foods is the deep-fried chocolate bar. Tasty – but very unhealthy! One fast food restaurant in Stonehaven on the east coast sells over three hundred deep-fried chocolate bars a week, mostly to children.

Cranachan – a traditional Scottish pudding

- 300 ml fresh double cream
- 30 g oatmeal
- 20 ml thick Scottish honey
- 20 ml Scotch whisky (optional)
- 500 g fresh raspberries

Cook the oatmeal in a frying pan until it is light brown. Whisk the cream with the whisky and the honey. Add in the oatmeal. Put the raspberries (except for four) into four small bowls. Put the cream with the oatmeal, whisky and honey on top of the raspberries. Finally put a raspberry on the top of each bowl.

ACTIVITIES

1 Are the sentences true (*T*) of false (*F*)?

1 Clans were not so important in the Highlands as in other parts of Scotland. $\boxed{F}$

2 People don't usually wear kilts every day. ☐

3 Tartan is only used for kilts. ☐

4 We know that bagpipes first came to Scotland from England. ☐

5 At a ceilidh, people usually sing and dance. ☐

6 On 25 January, the Scots have a special meal to remember the life of a poet. ☐

7 Hogmanay parties start on the first day of the year. ☐

8 Haggis is made with the inside parts of sheep. ☐

2 <u>Underline</u> the correct words in each sentence.

1 Scottish Gaelic is the <u>*oldest*</u> / *most spoken* language used in Scotland.

2 Today, Gaelic is spoken by *fewer / more* people than it was in the past.

3 Scottish Gaelic is similar to *English / Irish Gaelic*.

4 Most Gaelic speakers in Scotland live in *Glasgow / the Highlands and Islands*.

3 Answer the questions.

1 What type of music do the band Bodega play?

....

2 What instruments do Bodega play?

....

3 Which of the Scottish fast foods do you think sounds the nicest? Which do you think is the unhealthiest?

....

Chapter 3

Historic Scotland

One of the most important areas of Scottish history is the relationship between the Scots and the English. From very early times until the present day there have always been difficulties. In the past these difficulties often led to war. Today politicians don't fight, they argue.

The Romans, the English and the Scots ———

In 43 AD the Romans came to Britain. At first they stayed in the south of the country, but after some years they decided to move further north into Scotland. When they did, they had a difficult time. For four years they fought a war against the Scots, but it was not easy to find and catch the Scottish fighters in the hills and the mountains. In the end the Roman general, Agricola, took his soldiers[5] back to England.

Some years later another Roman emperor, Hadrian, decided it would be a good idea to keep the Scots and the English apart. In 122 AD he built a wall from west to east across the north of England. The idea was to stop the Scots coming into England. This wall, called Hadrian's Wall, is 117 kilometres long and took six years to build. It was about five metres high and three metres wide. They also built castles along the wall, where the soldiers could live.

For the next three hundred years there were Roman soldiers on Hadrian's Wall. They tried to keep the Scots out, but they were not always successful. Sometimes the Scots broke through the wall, and sometimes they just sailed around the end of it.

The Romans left Britain in the 5th century and Hadrian's Wall was never used again.

Today parts of the wall are still standing. Archaeologists have found many of the castles where Roman soldiers lived. You can visit these places and find out about the soldiers and what their life was like. You can walk along the top of the wall and look out on the land that Roman soldiers looked at. You can also walk along the complete length of the wall through some of Britain's most beautiful countryside.

War with England – William Wallace ────────

All through history, right up to the 18th century, the English and the Scots fought each other. One of the bloodiest times was at the beginning of the 14th century. There was no king of Scotland at the time. The king of England was Edward I and he was expecting the Scots to accept him as their king. Many of the important people in Scotland promised to accept Edward, but not a man called William Wallace. Wallace promised that he would do his best to kick the English out of Scotland. He did not want to be king himself. He just wanted Scotland to be a free country.

Wallace was a good fighter and a brave man. Many people agreed with him and joined his fight against the English. When King Edward heard about Wallace, he sent a large number of soldiers to Scotland. He wanted to fight the Scots and catch or kill Wallace.

Wallace was not just brave: he was clever too. He knew he did not have enough soldiers to fight the English and win. He realised he had to try something different. In 1297 he led his soldiers towards the English and met them at the River Forth, just outside the town of Stirling. Wallace stopped his men on a hill on one side of the river. The English were on the other side.

There was only a narrow bridge over the river and the English leader felt it was too dangerous for his soldiers to cross. He sent some men to talk to Wallace, but Wallace did not want to talk.

'We've come here to fight,' he said.

The English leader became angry at this and sent his soldiers across the bridge towards the Scots.

The Scots waited until half the English were across the river. Then they ran down the hill and attacked[6] them. Fighting half the English soldiers was much easier than fighting all of them and soon the Scots started to win. Before long, the English who had not crossed the river started to run away.

King Edward was fighting in France while this was happening. When he heard the news that the Scots had won at Stirling Bridge, he came back to England with the rest of his soldiers. Immediately he went north to Scotland himself. Again Wallace realised that he could not fight against so many English soldiers. Wallace's men stayed close to the English but only fought them if they met a small group.

Not everybody in Scotland liked Wallace. There were some rich and important people who had soldiers of their own and they decided to tell King Edward where to find Wallace. Then, when it became clear that the Scots and the English were going to fight, they did not allow their soldiers to fight with Wallace's army. With fewer soldiers than he expected, Wallace had no chance against the English. Many Scots lost their lives that day, including one of Wallace's best friends.

Wallace escaped into the mountains away from the English. He stayed free for some time, but in the end, in 1305, the English found out where he was. A man called Sir John de Menteith was happy to take a large bag of gold in return for telling the English where to find him.

The English took Wallace to London. King Edward knew that Scotland could never be his while Wallace was alive. He was tired and angry with Wallace and ordered him to be killed in a very unpleasant[7] way. Edward thought that would be the end of his problems in Scotland. But he was wrong.

Braveheart – How true was the film?

In 1995 Mel Gibson made the film *Braveheart* about the life of William Wallace. *Braveheart* is a good story: it was popular all round the world and especially in Scottish cinemas – but how true is it? The answer is that a lot was fact but not all. The biggest 'mistake' was the idea that there was a relationship between Wallace and Isabella, the wife of Edward II. The film also says that they had a child, who later became King Edward III. But in fact, at that time, Isabella was only three years old. And Edward III was not born until seven years after Wallace died!

War with England – Robert the Bruce ————

At this time there were two Scots who both wanted to be king: John Comyn and Robert the Bruce. John Comyn was well known, liked by many people and had fought hard against the English. Bruce had changed sides a number of times, sometimes fighting with the English, sometimes against them. He was not popular.

Although Comyn and Bruce reached an agreement that Bruce could become king, it was not long before they argued and Bruce killed Comyn. Bruce became king and so, less than a year after William Wallace's death, Scotland had a new king and the fight against the English continued.

Shortly after becoming king, Bruce was found by the English army together with his followers, and many of them were killed in the fighting. Bruce escaped to Ireland. Bruce thought that things were now hopeless, but one evening he was sitting on his own in an old house, looking up into the roof. He could see a spider trying to climb up to a piece of wood in the roof. As Bruce watched it, the spider started to climb but then fell back. It started again and failed again. And again. It tried and failed six times. But it continued trying, and the seventh time it reached the wood. Bruce stood up. The spider had given him hope. He decided to try again too.

Then Edward I died. This was good news for the Scots. Edward I had been a hard man and a strong king, but his son, also called Edward, was a weak man. Bruce and his followers returned to Scotland and started fighting the English again.

It was a long, slow fight, but little by little over the next eight years they won back land from the English. Like William Wallace, Bruce was careful never to fight all the English at the same time. He went from castle to castle, from town to town. He attacked small groups of English – but never all of them. He was a brave and clever fighter.

Then, in 1314, eight years after he had become king, Bruce decided it was time to make the English finally leave Scotland. King Edward II was in Scotland with a very large army. Bruce chose the time and place for the fight – Bannockburn, a small village near the town of Stirling. There the large English army lost to a small number of brave Scots. And Scotland was at last free from the English.

Famous Scots

Throughout history and in all areas of life there have been Scots whose names and work have been famous during their lifetime and have lived on after their death. From the 18th century, for example, come David Hume, the philosopher, and Adam Smith, the economist. From the 19th century there are the scientist John Clerk Maxwell and the explorer David Livingstone. Scientist and inventor Alexander Fleming and F1 motor racing champion Jackie Stewart are remembered from the 20th century. And among the famous Scots of today are actors Sean Connery, Kelly Macdonald, Tilda Swinton and Ewan McGregor. Other famous Scots include architects, writers, footballers, prime ministers, business people, engineers and tennis players.

Robert Louis Stevenson (1850–94) ———

TREASURE ISLAND
Robert Louis Stevenson

Robert Louis Stevenson is one of the best-known Scottish writers. His father and his grandfather were both famous lighthouse[8] engineers[9]. From them he got his love of travel and adventure.

Stevenson was not strong either as a child or as an adult. He was often ill. In fact, he was always searching for a place to live where the weather would be kind to his health.

Stevenson married an American woman, Fanny, when he was thirty. She was a great help to him when he was working. He often read his work to her and asked her what she thought. When he wrote one of his most famous books, *The Strange Case of Dr Jekyll and Mr Hyde*, Stevenson read her the story as usual. It was about a kind and intelligent doctor, Dr Jekyll, who turns into an ugly murdering monster, Mr Hyde, when he takes a special drug.

Fanny told him that there was a deeper meaning to the story which he had completely missed. She told him it was really about how everyone has both good and bad inside them. When he heard this, Stevenson realised she was right. He burned his story and wrote it again from start to finish in three days, this time using the idea that Fanny had given him.

After many years of travelling through France, Britain, the USA and the Pacific, Stevenson and his wife bought a house and land in Samoa, a group of islands in the middle of the Pacific Ocean. He died there at the age of forty-four.

James Watt (1736–1819)

One of Scotland's most famous inventors was James Watt. He was born near Glasgow in 1736. He was largely educated by his mother. When he was eighteen, his mother died and Watt went to London to learn how to make scientific instruments. He returned to Scotland a year later where he was employed at the University of Glasgow as an instrument maker. He became friends with some university professors and became interested in steam. Many people believe that James Watt invented the first steam engine.

Other Scottish inventions _____

Did you know that everything in the list below was invented by a Scot? Do you know who invented what? Match the person to the invention and then check your answers on page 80.

the detective Sherlock Holmes	Alexander Fleming
the bicycle	John Logie Baird
the car tyre	Arthur Conan Doyle
the telephone	John Boyd Dunlop
the medicine penicillin	Charles MacIntosh
the television	Kirkpatrick MacMillan
the raincoat	Alexander Graham Bell

England against Scotland – the present day ⎯

Today the only 'fighting' between England and Scotland happens on the sports fields. But in the world of Anglo-Scottish politics there are still areas where both Scottish and English people would like to see change.

Since the 17th century, England and Scotland have had just one king or queen for both countries. In the 18th century the English and the Scots decided to have just one government to look after both countries. However, at the end of the 20th century, the Scots began to feel that this should change. The British government asked the Scots to choose – and the Scots chose to have their own government.

In 1999 a Scottish government met for the first time for nearly three hundred years. They were not allowed to decide everything for the Scottish people, but they were able to make sure that many decisions about life in Scotland were made in Scotland. Life over the next few years looks interesting for the Scottish people.

ACTIVITIES

1 Use information from Chapter 3 to complete the timeline about Scottish history.

122 AD *the Roman emperor, Hadrian, starts building a wall*

1297 ....

1305 ....

1314 ....

1999 ....

2 Tick (✓) the sentences that are true for both William Wallace and Robert the Bruce.

1 He became king of Scotland. ☐
2 He wanted Scotland to be free of the English. ✓
3 He led Scottish soldiers in fights against the English. ☐
4 He escaped from the English. ☐
5 He was killed by the English. ☐
6 He wasn't popular with everyone in Scotland. ☐

3 Complete the sentences with the name *Robert Louis Stevenson* or *James Watt*.

1 *James Watt* lived in the 18th century.

2 .... was educated by his mother.

3 .... lived in the 19th century.

4 .... didn't have good health.

5 .... was helped in his work by his wife.

6 .... worked at a university.

7 .... lived in London.

8 .... lived on an island.

Chapter 4

Mysterious Scotland

Scotland has a long and rich history that reaches back to before the Romans came to Britain. During this time, many things have happened that are mysterious[10] or difficult to explain. Many places have stories about them that are hard, maybe even impossible, to believe.

The Rosslyn Chapel and *The Da Vinci Code*

In the middle of the 12th century in the sleepy village of Roslin, just south of Edinburgh, a man called William St Clair decided to build a church. Although he planned to build a large church, he died before the building was finished. Work stopped when he died and was never restarted. What is left therefore is a small church, or chapel, just 21 metres long and 10.5 metres wide.

The chapel has always been well known for its unusual and beautiful stonework. Both inside and outside the chapel are an amazing number of different stone figures: flowers, birds, leaves, plants, people's faces and also pictures of stories from religion.

Among the faces are those of two men who worked on the chapel. Their story is an interesting one. During the building of the chapel the leader of the stoneworkers did not know how to finish the part that he was working on. He went to Rome to find out what he had to do, but on his return he discovered that one of his students had finished the work for him. The leader was so jealous of the student's beautiful work that he killed him. The faces of these two men are among those in the chapel.

Another interesting thing about the different stone plants and leaves in the chapel is that some can only be found in North America. Some people believe that William St Clair's grandfather, a sailor called Prince Henry of Orkney, had travelled as far as America – over a hundred years before Christopher Columbus. The plants and leaves, they say, show that that story must be true.

The chapel has become even more famous since it played an important part in Dan Brown's best-selling book, *The Da Vinci Code*, which came out in 2003. The book sold over sixty million copies in the first three years and has been translated into forty-four languages. It has also been made into a film, starring Tom Hanks, Audrey Tautou and Sir Ian McKellen.

However, not everything that Dan Brown tells us about the chapel is completely true. For example, he says that there is a Star of David in the floor of the chapel, but there isn't one. He tells us it was built by the Knights Templar, but we know it was not.

Many books have been written about the chapel, especially in recent years. Because it is such an amazing and unusual building, there are many strange and different ideas about its importance. Some people think it is not just a place of religion, but that it is also a meeting place for a secret society. Others think it is a landing place for UFOs[11]. Some people believe there is something important to the Christian religion in the ground under the chapel. Could any of these ideas be right? Whatever the truth of the matter, the Rosslyn Chapel is a beautiful and interesting building.

Nessie – the Loch Ness monster _____

The most famous of the Scottish lakes is almost certainly Loch Ness. It is long and very deep. In fact, there is more water in Loch Ness than all the other lakes in Britain put together. Although the loch is set amongst beautiful mountains, not everyone goes there for the views. They go to see Nessie – the Loch Ness Monster.

From very early times people have talked of something strange living in the lake. But in the 1930s talk became real interest. The famous photo of Nessie above was taken by a doctor in 1934.

Since then there have been many photos and videos of Nessie and many people say they have seen the monster. A number of times scientists have tried to find out whether there really is a monster or not. In 1967 they tried with underwater sound waves; in the 1970s they tried with underwater photos; and in 1993 and 2001 they tried again with sound waves. Each time the scientists found something a little unusual – a strange photograph, sound waves showing something moving – but they were never able to show that there really is a monster. And Loch Ness is so big that they also could not say that there isn't a monster. So the mystery continues.

Of course, people think it is a good joke to make photos or videos to try and show that Nessie is real. The 1934 photo was very cleverly taken, but it was not really a photo of the monster. However, the joke was not discovered until sixty years later! In 2004 a television channel made a monster, like a dinosaur, that moved and looked real. Then they put it into Loch Ness. That day six hundred people said they had seen the monster.

Many people believe that there is no monster, but even the most disbelieving people take a quick look over the water – because you never know for sure …

The Fairy Flag of Dunvegan

On the west coast of the Isle of Skye stands Dunvegan Castle, the home of the chief, or leader, of the MacLeod clan. A long time ago the chief of the MacLeods married the woman who owned the castle and the MacLeods have lived at Dunvegan ever since.

At some time in the past – nobody knows exactly when – one of the chiefs of the MacLeods fell in love with a fairy[12] and asked her to marry him. She agreed on condition that, after twenty years, he would allow her to return home to her fairy land. One day, twenty years later, they were standing on a bridge near the castle. The fairy told her husband that it was time for him to keep his promise. He wanted her to stay so badly that he tried to stop her leaving. But she escaped from him, ran into some woods and was never seen again. He was left holding the cloth that she wore around her shoulders. That cloth is now called the Fairy Flag.

You can still see the Fairy Flag in a glass case on the wall in the castle. It is a very old, yellow piece of cloth. It is so old that it looks ready to fall to pieces if you even touch it. But it is the Fairy Flag and people say it is magical. The owners[13] of the flag can wave it to call for help from the fairies – but they can only do this three times. So far the MacLeods have waved the flag twice. The first time was many years ago when the MacLeods were fighting the MacDonalds and it seemed certain that the MacLeods were going to lose. The chief of the MacLeods waved the flag and from that moment on the MacLeods started to win the fight. The second time was when a young MacLeod child was ill and the family were afraid that he was going to die. They waved the flag again and the little boy lived.

During the Second World War pilots from the MacLeod clan all carried photos of the flag when they were flying. Not one of them was ever shot down.

There are, of course, other ideas about where the flag came from. One story is that it came from the Middle East in the 11th century and the MacLeods got it from soldiers who had fought there. In recent years a scientist from a British museum examined the flag carefully and explained to the chief of the MacLeods why he was sure it came from the Middle East.

'I'm afraid you are wrong,' the chief of the MacLeods told the scientist. 'I know for a fact that the fairies gave this flag to my family.'

'You clearly know much more about it than I do, sir,' replied the scientist seriously. 'You must be right.'

Maybe the chief of the MacLeods was right and it *did* come from the fairies.

The flag has not yet been waved for the third and last time.

Castles

The first castles were built in Scotland in the 11th and 12th centuries. They were built to live in but also to keep out people who were not friendly. How many castles are there in Scotland today? Over two thousand castles have been built, but some have disappeared and we only know about them from land records. At least 250 castles have their own website on the Internet – but many do not. What are today's castles like? What can you do in them? Well, some castles are privately owned and they are kept private. You cannot go into them at all. But what about the others?

Airth Castle was built in the 14th century and was first owned by the Erth family. Through the years it has often changed owners, at

You can have a holiday at Airth Castle

44

one time belonging to the family of Robert the Bruce, who was king of Scotland in the 14th century. The castle became a hotel in 1971. It has 120 bedrooms, a restaurant, a swimming pool and a gym[14] … a great place for a holiday!

Huntly Castle, near Aberdeen, was first built out of wood at the end of the 12th century. At the beginning of the 15th century this castle became the home of the Gordon clan. Lord Gordon pulled down the old wooden castle and built a stone one in its place.

In 1649 the Gordon clan was fighting against the government. The chief of the clan was caught and killed by government soldiers. For the next 150 years no one lived in the castle. Then in 1799 the roof was taken off and the windows taken out; the castle was allowed to fall to pieces.

You can think about what Huntly Castle used to be like

The first part of Lauriston Castle in Edinburgh was built in the 16th century. A large new part was added in the 19th

century. A number of famous Scots have lived here. The last owners left the castle to be looked after by the government. The inside of the castle is exactly as it was when the last owner died in 1926. Visitors can go round the castle and see how the owners lived.

You can see how people used to live at Lauriston Castle.

Traquair House near Edinburgh is the oldest castle in Scotland that people still live in. It was built in 1107 and twenty-seven Scottish kings and queens have stayed in it. You can go round the castle on your own, or sometimes the owner, Lady Maxwell Stuart, gives tours. You can find out from her what it is really like to live in a castle.

You can see how people still live in Traquair House.

Castles and ghosts ————————————

Some Scottish castles have histories, often bloody ones, going back over six hundred years. It is no surprise then to discover that there are many stories of ghosts, strange noises and unusual happenings. At the famous Culzean Castle, owned by the Kennedy family, the ghost of a piper plays in the grounds when one of the family is about to get married. At Castle Fraser there is not exactly a ghost. However, in the 19th century a young woman was murdered and her body was pulled down the stairs. It is said that blood kept appearing on the stone stairs, no matter how hard people tried to clean it off. At Dunrobin Castle in the north of Scotland the ghost of a woman appears on the upper floors of the castle. People say it is the daughter of one of the owners of the castle. He locked her in a room at the top of the castle to stop her from marrying someone he did not like. The woman tried to escape out of the window but fell to her death. There are at least 150 castles in Scotland where people think there are ghosts.

Findhorn

In 1962 Peter and Eileen Caddy, their three children and their friend, Dorothy Maclean, arrived at a campsite in Findhorn, a small village on the coast of northeast Scotland. Peter, Eileen and Dorothy were unusual people with unusual ideas. They had little money and no jobs, so Peter decided to grow vegetables. Dorothy had some special ideas on how to grow vegetables in difficult conditions. Soon, although the ground was dry and sandy, they were growing amazingly large plants, flowers and vegetables. One of their cabbages[15] weighed ten kilos!

The news of this amazing garden got out. Scientists came and could not believe it. Other people, who shared the same ideas and philosophy as Dorothy Maclean and the Caddys, came to stay. The campsite started to become a small village of its own where people tried to live in a deeper and more caring way.

Today Findhorn is home to about three hundred people. It also provides a centre for others who live in the wider community. Throughout the year courses are held at Findhorn. On these courses, students can look at education, ecology, ways of living and other important ideas shared by the Findhorn community. The courses are not just for adults; there are special courses for families and for teenagers too.

ACTIVITIES

1 Complete the sentences with the names of the places in the box.

> Rosslyn Chapel (x2) Loch Ness (x2)
> Dunvegan Castle Findhorn

1 _Rosslyn Chapel_ has pictures of a murderer and the man he killed as part of its decoration.

2 .... plays a part in a famous book.

3 .... is home to a Scottish clan chief.

4 .... is where a famous photo was taken in 1934.

5 .... is home to people who have special ideas about how to live.

6 .... may have something strange living in it.

2 Are the sentences true (*T*) or false (*F*)?

1 Airth Castle used to belong to a Scottish King's family and is now a hotel. ☐T

2 The Gordon clan still live at Huntly Castle. ☐

3 Lauriston Castle looks the same inside as it did in the 1920s. ☐

4 Nobody lives in Traquair House today. ☐

5 There is a musical ghost at Culzean Castle. ☐

3 Answer the questions.

1 What is unusual about the stone plants and leaves in the Rosslyn Chapel?

....

2 What happened in 1967, 1993 and 2001 at Loch Ness?

....

49

Sporting Scotland

The back pages of Scotland's newspapers are always full of news about football, football clubs and footballers, but football is not a traditional Scottish sport. There are two sports that are special to Scotland: curling and golf. Surprisingly it seems that more Scots play golf than football. Curling is played by far fewer people. However, as you will see below, the Scots are good at it.

Curling

Curling is a game played on ice. It is an unusual game. There are four people in a curling team: the leader of the team, called the skip, and three others. One of the team throws something, called a stone, along the ice; he or she is trying to get the stone to the middle of a circle, called the target or house, about forty metres away. Two of the other players sweep the ice with long brushes to make the stone go faster or slower, or to the left or the right. The skip tells the sweepers what to do. Each team is trying to get its stones nearer to the middle of the circle than the other team's stones.

No one knows for certain where the game started: maybe in Scotland, maybe in Holland. However, it is true to say that the game has a long history in Scotland, beginning in the 16th century, and it is the Scots who introduced it to other cold parts of the world where the game is now played, for example, Canada, Sweden and Russia. By the second half of the 18th century thousands of people were enjoying the sport and almost every town had its own curling pond. Today there are well over six hundred curling clubs in Scotland and the sport is played by over fifteen thousand people of all ages.

Scotland wins world junior gold

Scotland won its second junior women's title, beating Sweden 12–3 at the World Junior Curling Championships.

Seventeen-year-old Eve Muirhead and her team of Kerry Barr, Vicki Adams, Kay Adams and Sarah MacIntyre had already lost two games to Sweden's Cissi Ostlund earlier in the week, including losing 8–2 in Saturday's semi-final. But in the final, it was a different story as Scotland led from start to finish, beating Sweden comfortably.

Muirhead and MacIntyre were also in the Scotland team that won the Junior World Championships last year. 'It feels really good,' said Muirhead after the match. 'We knew early on if we could just stay on top of things, we'd be fine.'

Golf

St Andrews golf club

Most people believe that golf began in Scotland some time during the 15th century. There is a record of King James II ordering the Scots not to play golf: they were spending too much time playing golf and not enough time training for war. However, fifty years later, King James IV became interested in the sport and it was soon introduced into England and France.

The first golf club started in Scotland in the 17th century and the first one outside Scotland in the 18th century. Soon the golf club at St Andrews on the east coast of Scotland became the most important club in the country and quickly it turned into the centre of the golfing world.

'Golf has more rules than any other game because golf has more cheaters than any other game.'
– *Bruce Lansky, American writer*

Junior competition may be first of many

The first ever European tournament for the world's best young junior golfers will start next week at four courses near Edinburgh. Young Scottish children aged between seven and fourteen will compete against players from thirty-four other countries around the world.

For the first time the US Kids Golf Foundation has organised a competition in Europe and, if all goes well, it could be a competition that happens every year.

Dan Van Horn, President of US Kids Golf, believes the competition will be a great chance for young golfers from all over the world to show what they can do.

Fourteen-year-old Donald MacLeish, from Gullane, knows he will have to be lucky to win. He hopes that playing on his home course will be a help – but above all he just wants to enjoy the experience.

'It will be good to play people from other countries, but I really just want to play well.'

When asked why the competition would be in Scotland, Alisdair Good, one of the competition organisers from the Gullane Golf Club, answered simply, 'It is the home of golf.'

Tennis brothers

Although tennis is in no way a Scottish sport, Andy Murray and his elder brother, Jamie, are very much the new faces of the sport in Scotland. Born in 1986 and 1987, the Murray brothers were introduced to tennis at an early age by their mother, Judy, who was a tennis coach. While they were growing up, tennis was not the boys' only sporting interest: Andy was keen on football and Jamie was a good golfer.

At home in Dunblane, central Scotland, Andy had only his brother to practise against. He realised that by going somewhere else he could practise against better players. So, at the age of fifteen, Andy made the important decision to go abroad to train. Andy went to Barcelona where he trained at a famous Spanish tennis school. It was a good move. Two years later he won the Junior Competition at the US Open. In 2008 he reached the final of the US Open.

Jamie Murray decided to do things differently. He became a doubles player. And although Andy Murray is the better player, it was Jamie who was the first to win at Wimbledon. In 2007 he won the mixed doubles competition with Jelena Jankovic.

For both Andy and Jamie, there is still a long way to go. At times they both play some of the most exciting tennis you will see. However, there is still much hard work to do if they are to get to the very top of their sport. That is certainly where they would both like to be – so you will almost certainly be hearing and reading a lot more about the Murray brothers.

Highland Games

A Highland Games is a day of traditional sporting competitions held all across Scotland through the summer months in cities, towns and villages. There are a number of different competitions. There are piping and dancing competitions, running competitions, and there are the 'heavy' competitions, which test how strong people are. Among the 'heavy' competitions are the 'tug-of-war', where two teams see which can pull the hardest; and 'tossing the caber', in which people see how far they can throw a tall and heavy piece of wood called a 'caber'.

Most of the competitions have different age groups so that both young people and older people can all enter. People who live in the area near the games will enter, but both Scottish and

tug-of-war

foreign athletes travel round the country during the summer entering competitions at different games. There are prizes to be won! If you're in Scotland in the summer, make sure you go to a Highland Games – you might win a prize.

tossing the caber

Celtic Football Club

In 1967 Glasgow Celtic was the first British team to become European Champions, beating Inter Milan 2–1 in Lisbon. Each of the eleven Celtic players in that match was born within fifty kilometres of Parkhead, the Celtic football ground. In today's Celtic team you might find players from six or seven different countries.

Mountain boarding – the sport of the future?

Snowboarding is OK, but you need snow and it is cold. Skateboarding is fun, but you need somewhere flat and it hurts when you fall off. Surfing? In Scotland? You must be crazy! The sea is much too cold. But take a little bit of each, mix them up with a bit of mountain biking, and you've got the sport of the future – mountain boarding! What's more, a mountain board goes anywhere: streets, hills, dirt roads, wherever you want.

This new sport, which started in American ski resorts during the summer months, is the latest sporting fashion to hit Scotland.

A mountain board looks like a big skateboard with wheels on the end of the board instead of under it. The wheels are larger than on a skateboard and boards cost anywhere from €200 to €700.

To stay safe it is a good idea to wear a helmet[16] and covers for your knees, elbows and wrists. If

you're a mad downhill racer, you may want even more than that.

Mountain boarding is fun and exciting; the people who do it are friendly and will always help beginners. Find somewhere safe to start, don't do anything unnecessarily dangerous, and you will really enjoy your mountain boarding experience.

ACTIVITIES

1 Match the facts about sports in Scotland with the sports in the box.

> curling (x3)   golf (x3)   mountain boarding
> tossing the caber

1 It's a good idea to wear a helmet for this sport. _mountain boarding_
2 In the past, people were ordered not to play it. ....
3 It began during the 15th century. ....
4 There are four people in a team. ....
5 It began in the 16th century. ....
6 A long, heavy piece of wood is used in this sport. ....
7 It's played on ice. ....
8 There is a famous centre for this sport on the east coast of Scotland. ....

2 Complete the news about sport and sportspeople with information from Chapter 5.

1 _Eve Muirhead_ and her team won the World Junior Curling Championships with a score of 12–3 against 2................................. .

Fourteen-year-old golfer Donald 3................................. hopes to win the European Junior Golf Tournament. There will be players there from 4................................. different countries.

5................................. , the Scottish tennis player, won the US Open Junior Competition in 6................................. . His brother 7................................. won the Wimbledon mixed doubles competition in 8................................. with Jelena Jankovic.

Chapter 6

Dark Scotland

Not everything about Scotland is bright and sunny. The weather for one thing can be cold, wet and windy, even in summer. And there are also some dark stories: stories of lies, criminals and murderers.

The man who wanted to be king

Macbeth is a famous story by the English writer, William Shakespeare. Macbeth, who lived in the 11th century, was a good soldier. One day, while coming back from fighting, he met three old women. These women told him that they could look into the future and they each told him one thing that would happen to him. The last woman told him that he would become king of Scotland.

At first Macbeth did not believe the old women, but, later, the first two things that they had told him came true. There was only one thing left – they had told him he would become king. The king at that time, Macbeth's boss, was a man called Duncan. Macbeth started to think about killing Duncan so that he could become king. However, Macbeth was not sure. Duncan had been good to Macbeth and he was also his cousin. Macbeth told his wife about the old women and also about his thoughts of killing Duncan. Lady Macbeth hated Duncan and wanted to be queen. She became angry with her husband, calling him a weak man, until finally Macbeth decided to kill Duncan.

After Duncan's death, Duncan's sons and their friend Macduff escaped to England and Macbeth became king. At first Macbeth was a good king. However, after some time he started to worry about his future, so he went to see the old women again. They told him he would be safe until Great Birnam Wood came to Dunsinane Hill. Macbeth felt much happier at this because the wood and the hill were twenty kilometres apart. But just to make sure that he would be safe, he built a strong castle on Dunsinane Hill.

In England at this time Duncan's sons and Macduff started to plan their return to Scotland. They got together a large number of soldiers and started north. When they reached Great Birnam Wood, Macduff told the soldiers to cut off branches and other pieces of the trees to hold in front of them. This would make it difficult for Macbeth to see how many soldiers were coming.

The soldiers moved on towards Dunsinane Hill. When Macbeth saw them coming with the pieces of the trees from Birnam Wood, he knew he was in trouble. However, he was a brave man and led his soldiers out to fight. During the fighting he was killed by Macduff.

'The Scottish play'

William Shakespeare's story of Macbeth is not true. There was a Scottish king called Macbeth. He *did* become king after Duncan and he *was* killed by the English. However, everything else that Shakespeare tells us is just a story.

Many actors all over the world believe that it brings bad luck to say the name *Macbeth* unless you are actually acting in the play. That's why you will hear actors talking about 'the Scottish play' and not *Macbeth*. Nobody knows whether it really does bring bad luck, but certainly some strange things have happened.

- The actor who played Lady Macbeth in the very first performance suddenly became ill and died.
- At one theatre where the play was showing, the director of the play and one of the actors were in a car accident. Then, some time later, the owner of the theatre died.
- In 1971 at a theatre in New York, there were two fires and seven robberies during the time the play was showing.

Glencoe – Scotland's darkest hour _____

Throughout the 17th century there was fighting in Scotland: fighting between different clans, and fighting between the king's soldiers and people who wanted a different king. In those days there was a lot of fighting everywhere.

Towards the end of the century King William III decided to pardon any clans who had fought against him, as long as they made a promise of friendship before New Year's Day the following year. The chief of the MacDonald clan took a long time to decide. Finally he decided he had to make the promise, so he went to the nearest town to do so. When he arrived there, he discovered it was the wrong town. He had to travel further and he arrived late – on 6 January.

He was allowed to make the promise and returned home, thinking that everything was OK and that his people were safe. But the government in Scotland had other ideas. They wanted to make an example of someone and they thought the MacDonalds were just right.

A group of about 130 soldiers led by Captain Robert Campbell was sent to Glencoe, the home of the MacDonalds. The soldiers were told they were going to get some money that the MacDonalds had to pay the government. The soldiers arrived at Glencoe and the MacDonalds, being Highlanders, gave them food and beds. The soldiers stayed for thirteen days and during that time the Highlanders made them feel welcome.

Then orders arrived from the government that the soldiers should kill all the MacDonalds under the age of seventy. At five o'clock the next morning the soldiers rose up and started killing the MacDonalds. Thirty-eight MacDonalds died; another forty escaped into the hills only to die later from cold or because they had no food.

Because the Campbell and the MacDonald clans often fought, many people believed this was just another clan fight. But this was not true. It was murder by government soldiers. And the crime seemed even worse because the MacDonalds had looked after the soldiers so well in their homes for so long.

Glencoe is one of the most beautiful places in the west of Scotland: high rocky mountains running down to the blue waters of the sea. When dark clouds come in low over the mountains this seems to be a truly strange place; and even in bright sunlight the visitor can feel that something terrible happened here.

Scotland's most famous murderers ─────────

In the early 1800s two Irishmen, William Burke and William Hare, came to live in Edinburgh. William Hare ran a small hotel where Burke and his girlfriend, Helen MacDougal, and other people stayed. By day Burke and Hare seemed to be good, hard-working men. But at night it was a very different story.

It all began when one of the guests in William Hare's house fell ill and died. At this time in Edinburgh a lot of people were studying medicine. The university needed dead bodies that students could cut up for examination. In the early 19th century, universities were only allowed to use the bodies of dead murderers and there were not enough. Hare knew this and so he and Burke took the body of the dead guest to Professor Robert Knox at the Edinburgh College of Medicine. Knox paid them well for the body and did not ask them where it had come from.

When another guest fell ill, Burke and Hare saw the chance to make some more easy money. This time, however, they did not wait for the man to die. They got him drunk on whisky and then killed him. Over the next two years Burke and Hare killed at least another fifteen people, possibly as many as thirty. They used to hold the person down and then cover his or her nose and mouth. There would therefore be no strange marks on the body when they took it to Professor Knox. In the beginning they killed only people who would not be missed: people who lived on the street, people who had few friends. But they soon became greedy.

WILLIAM BURKE   WILLIAM HARE

They murdered a woman called Mary Haldane. When Mary's daughter, Peggy, came round to ask Burke and Hare if they had seen her mother, they killed her too. However, Peggy Haldane was well known in the area and people realised that she had gone missing. Next they killed a young boy called Jamie. He was also well known and when Professor Knox uncovered the body in class the next morning, several of his students knew who it was. The professor immediately cut off the head and feet and told everyone that it was not Jamie.

Finally they killed a woman called Mary Doherty who Burke had invited to the guesthouse. Two of the other guests in the house, James and Ann Gray, realised that something was wrong. They looked round the house and discovered Mary Doherty's body. Burke offered the Grays money not to go to the police, but they would not take it. When the police came to the house, they could not find the body. Then they went to Professor Knox and found that he had it.

It was difficult for the police to show that Burke and Hare had actually killed anyone. After a month of questioning the police were getting nowhere, so they reached an agreement with Hare. If he told them that Burke was the murderer, then he could go free. Hare accepted the offer and went free.

Hare's wife and Burke's girlfriend were also freed because the police could not show that they knew anything about the murders. Professor Knox did not go to prison either. It could not be shown that he knew where the bodies came from. However, Burke was found guilty of murder and was hanged in January 1829. His body was given to the Edinburgh College of Medicine and his skeleton[17] can still be seen today in their library.

ACTIVITIES

1 Put the sentences about Macbeth in order.

1 He builds a castle. ☐
2 Two things that the women told him come true. ☐
3 He kills King Duncan. ☐
4 He loses the fight against King Duncan's sons and Macduff. ☐
5 He tells his wife what the last woman told him. ☐
6 Three women tell him three things that are going to happen to him. ☐ 1

2 Are the sentences true (*T*) or false (*F*)?

1 The MacDonald clan chief made a promise too late. ☐ T
2 The MacDonalds weren't kind to the king's soldiers. ☐
3 Not all the MacDonalds were killed by the king's soldiers. ☐
4 Burke and Hare killed the first person whose body they sold to Professor Knox. ☐
5 At first, Burke and Hare didn't kill people who were known in the area. ☐
6 Hare went free because he told the police that Burke was the murderer. ☐

3 Answer the questions.

1 What bad luck has 'the Scottish play' brought? Write one example.

....

2 What can a visitor to Glencoe feel about the past?

....

3 How did Burke and Hare make the murders seem like normal deaths?

....

4 What happened to William Burke's body?

....

Chapter 7

Urban Scotland

Although Scotland is a land of wide open spaces, mountains and beautiful islands, around eighty percent of the population live in urban[18] areas. Edinburgh and Glasgow are the two main cities, followed by Aberdeen. Other Scottish cities are rather small. They are really no bigger than towns. However, here we look at the three main cities in Scotland.

Edinburgh

Edinburgh is the capital of Scotland. It is also one of the most beautiful cities in Europe. The main street, Princes Street, has shops on only one side, with gardens and the castle on the other. Edinburgh Castle, high on a hill in the Old Town, looks over the city from the centre; Arthur's Seat, a high green hill, looks over it from the southeast. The New Town, which is actually almost 250 years old, has wide streets and beautiful 17th-century buildings.

In August and September every year Edinburgh has an arts festival. There are shows for adults, shows for teenagers and shows for children. There are films, plays and musicals. There are comedians, bands and singers. You can see shows in cinemas, theatres, church halls and the castle – even shows in the street.

But it is not just at festival time that Edinburgh comes alive. Throughout the year there is always something happening. There is a large student population: it has three universities and many other colleges. Many teenagers and young adults from other countries go to Edinburgh to learn English. There are cinemas and theatres, both large and small. There are clubs and pubs. There is the National Museum of Scotland and the National Gallery of Scotland. It has all the advantages of a capital city – yet the open countryside is only twenty minutes away by car.

Scottish parliament building

In 1999 work started on a building for the new Scottish government. The building was planned by a Spanish Catalan architect, Enric Miralles, who sadly died before it was finished. There were many problems during the building work. The building company said it would take two years to build – it took five! They said it would cost between £10 and £40 million – in the end it cost £414 million! And when the building was finally completed, some people loved it – but some people hated it!

Glasgow

Bigger than Edinburgh, Glasgow is probably Scotland's 'coolest[19]' city. Glaswegians, the people from Glasgow, certainly think so! In Glasgow there is something for all the family, from museums like the Burrell Collection for those who like art, to the Scottish National Football Museum for sports fans. You can find out about Glasgow's past at the People's Palace or look into the future

at the Glasgow Science Centre. You can visit the Glasgow School of Art, a building designed by the famous Scottish designer, Charles Rennie Mackintosh. You can go to a concert at the Clyde Auditorium, known locally as the Armadillo – just look at it and you will see why. Or you can go shopping along busy Sauchiehall Street. There is a busy nightlife with pubs, clubs, restaurants, cinemas and theatres, where you can meet and chat[20] to the locals. And, as Glaswegians will be sure to tell you, they are the friendliest people in Scotland.

Aberdeen

Aberdeen is Scotland's third-largest city with a population of just over 200,000. It is in the cold northeast corner of Scotland and it is a city that people either love or hate. Those who hate it describe it as grey, cold and unwelcoming. It is true that the city is grey: it is often called 'the Granite City' because most of the buildings are made out of grey granite stone. It is also true that the weather can be bad: the city is further north than Moscow and there is often snow, icy rain and strong winds. And the grey and cold make it seem unwelcoming. However, that is not the full story.

Aberdeen is one of the cleanest cities in Britain. Also, almost any open space seems to be a park: there are beautiful flower gardens and green areas in all parts of the city. There is a busy harbour. There are fantastic museums and art galleries. There are theatres, concert halls, cinemas and clubs. It has the best beach of any large city in Britain – though only a brave person goes swimming that far north in the North Sea! And since the 1970s Aberdeen has been the 'oil' city of Britain. Oil from the North Sea has brought money and people to Aberdeen, making it a busy, exciting place.

City or country, castle or croft, mountain or loch, there is so much to enjoy about Scotland. Its history is rich and interesting; its traditions alive and colourful. There are dark stories in the past of bloody fights and murders, but the Scotland of today is an exciting country looking forward to a bright future. Its people are friendly and generous – do not believe people who may tell you something different! It is a country that has moved into the 21st century with hope and promise.

The rose of all the world is not for me. I want for my part
Only the little white rose of Scotland
That smells sharp and sweet – and breaks the heart.
— *Hugh MacDiarmid (Christopher Murray Grieve)*
1892–1978, Scottish poet

ACTIVITIES

1 Match the facts about cities in Scotland with the places in the box.

> Aberdeen   Edinburgh   Glasgow

1 In the centre of this city there is a castle on a hill. *Edinburgh*
2 There is a building in this city that was designed by a famous Scottish designer. ....
3 It is known for being cold and grey. ....
4 It has a nice beach, but you may not want to swim here. ....
5 People in this city consider themselves to be very friendly. ....
6 There is a festival for people of all ages held here in late summer. ....
7 There are three universities in this city. ....
8 It's a very clean city. ....
9 The countryside is very near this city. ....
10 This city has lots of green areas. ....

2 Answer the questions.

1 Do most people in Scotland live in towns or the countryside?
....

2 What is there for people to do in Edinburgh?
....

3 What different kinds of museums can you visit in Glasgow?
....

4 What happened in Aberdeen in the 1970s?
....

5 What does the author say about the future of Scotland?
....

Glossary

[1]**traditional** (page 5) *adjective*   following the ways of behaving that have continued in a group of people for a long time without changing

[2]**lamb** (page 16) *noun*   a young sheep

[3]**pattern** (page 21) *noun*   a design of lines, colours, etc.

[4]**coal** (page 23) *noun*   a hard, black material that you find in the ground and burn to produce heat

[5]**soldier** (page 27) *noun*   a person whose job is to fight

[6]**attack** (page 30) *verb*   to use violence to hurt someone or something

[7]**unpleasant** (page 31) *adjective*   not nice

[8]**lighthouse** (page 34) *noun*   a tall building with a large light which shows ships where there is danger

[9]**engineer** (page 34) *noun*   a person who designs or builds machines, roads, etc.

[10]**mysterious** (page 39) *adjective*   strange and not explained or understood

[11]**UFO** (page 40) *noun*   (Unidentified Flying Object) a flying object which people think comes from another planet

[12]**fairy** (page 43) *noun*   a small person, often with wings, who is not real and has special powers

[13]**owner** (page 43) *noun*   if you are the **owner** of something, it belongs to you

[14]**gym** (page 45) *noun*   a room or building where you can do exercise

[15]**cabbage** (page 48) *noun*   a large, round vegetable with a lot of green or white leaves

[16]**helmet** (page 58) *noun*   a strong hard hat that covers and protects the head

[17]**skeleton** (page 68) *noun*   the bones that hold the body of a person or animal

[18]**urban** (page 70) *adjective*   of or in a city or town

[19]**cool** (page 72) *adjective*   good or in fashion

[20]**chat** (page 73) *verb*   to talk with someone in a friendly way

Inventions – answers from page 36

The detective Sherlock Holmes was 'invented' by Arthur Conan Doyle.

The bicycle was invented by Kirkpatrick MacMillan.

The car tyre was invented by John Boyd Dunlop. You can still buy Dunlop tyres.

The telephone was invented by Alexander Graham Bell.

The medicine penicillin was invented by Alexander Fleming.

The television was invented by John Logie Baird.

The raincoat was invented by Charles MacIntosh. That is why people often call a raincoat a 'mac'.

The authors and publishers are grateful to the following for permission to use copyright material. All efforts have been made to contact the copyright holders of material reproduced in this book which belongs to third parties, and citations are given for the sources. We welcome approaches from any copyright holders whom we have not been able to trace but who find that their material has been reproduced herein.

p5 istockphoto.com/©Stephen Finn (bridge) & Iain Sarjeant (cottage); p7 istockphoto.com/©Matt Tilghman; p8 istockphoto.com/©Steve Elsworth; p9 istockphoto.com/©Derek Dammann; p11 murdophoto.com; p12 shutterstock/©Joe Gough; p13 istockphoto.com/©Joe Gough; p14 ©David Robertson; p15 istockphoto.com/©Roger Whiteway (deer)/©Chris Crafter (otter)/©David P. Lewis (squirrel)/©Alexander Hafemann (puffin) & ©Inga Brennan–Photography & Design (eagle); pp 16–7 ©scottishislandexplorer; pp 20–1 shutterstock/©Nic Neish (tartans) & istockphoto.com/©Ron Sumners (piper); p22 Davie Gardner; p24 istockphoto.com/©Dirk Richter (bottles)/©Joanne Green (haggis); p25 shutterstock/©Monkey Business Images (cranachan); p28 istockphoto.com/©Duncan Gilbert; p29 istockphoto.com/©Allan Crawford; p31 CORDONPRESS; p32 istockphoto.com/©HultonArchive; p34 Time & Life Pictures/Getty Images (Watt) & istockphoto.com/©David Palmer (steam engine); p35 ©The Stevenson House Collection, Monterey, California State Parks; p40 shutterstock/©Chad Bontrager; p41 Keystone/Getty Images; p44 ©mysterious-scotland.com; p45 shutterstock/©Paul Butchard; p46 ©mysterious-scotland.com; p48 ©Findhorn Foundation; p50 istockphoto.com/©Allan Morrison; p51 ©scottishcurler.com; p52 bigstockphoto/©fintastique; p53 istockphoto.com/©Reuben Schulz; p54 ©Hou Jun/Xinhua Press/Corbis; p55 ©Leo Mason/Corbis; p56 istockphoto.com/©graham heywood; p57 ©Alan Crawford (caber) & Popperfoto/Getty Images (Celtic FC); p58 bigstockphoto/©christophriddle; p59 istockphoto.com/©Matthew Barnett; p61 istockphoto.com/©Ron Summers; p63 shutterstock/©Justin Kirk Thornton; p66 istockphoto.com/©Mike Bentley; p67 Courtesy of the New York Academy of Medicine Library; p70 istockphoto.com/©Chris Hepburn; p71 shutterstock/©Stephen Finn; p72 shutterstock/©Duirinish Light; p73 istockphoto.com/©David Woods (Armadillo); p74 istockphoto.com/©Adrian Beesley; p75 istockphoto.com/©onfilm; p76 istockphoto.com/©Bernd Seiffert

pp 16–7 Thanks to the *Scottish Island Explorer* for Eilidh MacFadyen's story